Silence, No More

Liz Moore

Copyright © 2020 Elizabeth "Liz" Moore

All rights reserved.

ISBN 978-0-9999066-0-6

No part of this publication may be reproduced, distributed, or transmitted in any form or by any means, including photocopying, recording, or other electronic or mechanical methods, without the prior written permission of the publisher, except in the case of brief quotations embodied in critical reviews and certain other noncommercial uses permitted by copyright law. For permission requests, write to the publisher, addressed "Attention: Permissions Coordinator," at the address below.

Editor-in-Chief:
Christina M. Berard LMHC, LCDP, MAC
Author, Poet & Editor | www.christinaberard.me

Publisher:
Ten19 Media Group for Artist Jerrell Grimes, LLC
Tampa Bay, Florida | www.ten19media.com

Ordering Information:
Quantity sales. Special discounts are available on quantity purchases by corporations, associations, and others. For details, contact the publisher at the e-mail, phone or fax below.

Orders by U.S. trade bookstores and wholesalers. Please contact Ten19 Media Group: Tel: (813) 205-4601; Fax: (833) 823-0237 or e-mail: ten19mediagroup@gmail.com

Printed in the United States of America.

About the Author

Liz Moore was born and raised in Brooklyn, New York. She currently resides in Providence, RI with her husband and two sons. She enjoys music, dancing, reading and staying healthy. She also enjoys helping and mentoring young adults. She has worked in the field of social work, in addition to being an advocate and mentor, for over twenty-five years. She loves empowering others.

Liz has been writing for over 15 years. Her real-life experiences, her love for poetry, journaling, and writing short stories, has given her a wide range of topics to share and write about.

Liz would like to encourage her readers to remember no matter where you have started, or where you may find yourself you can overcome adversity.

A special thank you...

My mother, Maxine, for always encouraging me to be awesome; both of my sons, Ramel and Alex Jr., who gave me reasons to live life, and taught me what love truly is; lastly, but certainly not least, my soulmate, best friend and husband, Alexander Moore. I am truly blessed to have you in my life. I am your rib, and you are my Adam. Your encouragement kept me writing.

A message from the Author

For those who are not aware of the higher power or even those who don't believe, I would like to take this time to introduce the one who has blessed me and brought me through every journey in my life.

I must admit I did not grow up knowing who my savior, the Lord Jesus Christ, was and how much he would play the major role in my life, until I was an adult. God has blessed me with the talent to write and the courage to put my imagination on paper for the world to be inspired and blessed.

Still I must say to those who did not believe in me and tried to discourage me, I wish you well.

And to you, my readers: I hope you read this and learn the lesson that has been written just for you in the pages of this book. Most importantly, don't let anybody discourage you. Criticism can motivate you as long as you don't allow it to break you. A little hope and faith can go a long way. I am living proof that you can and will reach your destiny.

God, I give you all the glory for placing all of those wonderful and not-so-kind people in my life. I pray blessings on everyone who reads my book.

Silence, No More.

Table of Contents

A message from the Author.....5

Reaping Love....11

Even Now, Life Is Not My Own....13

Nothing to Me...15

Yours....17

One Ending....19

It's Over...21

Love of My Life (Short Story) 23

Life....39

Don't Let Him Get Yours!.43

Found Not Guilty....45

Goodbye Darkness....49

Far Behind....51

Broken Pieces....55

Family Ties (Short Story) 59

I Have Finally Arrived....67

Not Lost or Forgotten....69

True Story....71

His Name is Jesus Christ....75

Inside Out....77

Hired for a Reason....79

Drive It Into Self....83

Mysterious Man....85

A Healed Heart....87

Remember, I Love You....89

Rhetorical...91

Broken (Short Story) 93

Remember, We Are One....101

Until the End of The World....103

No Surrender, No Retreat....105

Silence, No More

Liz Moore

Long and lonely was my road

I have for years reaped nothing but this feeling

Is that what I have to call my own?

My heart has been sentenced to years locked behind this steel gate

I have lost all hope, and then I met one who says he

has the plans for my heart's great escape

He tells me I won't be made a fool

I tell you I want to believe, but I'm a little scared

I don't want to be caught in a snare

However, I will be with him; I will follow his plan to the end

Wherever the end will be, so will I with him

and the hopes that he is the one

He holds the key to set me free

I have been locked behind a steel gate of fear

Sowing something new

Reaping love

I remember the day so very well

Only my story I can tell

you

from the beginning to the end

What happened is what everyone wants to know

She was a girl

A black girl

Growing up in a racist world

With mountains of problems that were gifts from all those around her

Hills of fears they knew she could never climb

Victim she became after the very first rape

That tore into her soul deeper than rivers and wider than seas

Hands touching her body where they should not have been

at the precious age of ten

Trying to block out every memory of the suffering and the pain

Inflicted by him, by her

I knew I would never be the same

"Struggle" became my middle name, trying to undo the pain

Searching for who "she" really is

Loving herself became almost impossible

Even now, my life is not my own

I like who I am

Regardless of your feelings for me

I like what I stand for

Even if you don't do anything but complain

as you sit

I love the way I look, the shade of my skin, the curves in my hips

No, you can't see with blinded eyes,

my beauty

It comes to no surprise

My spirit and soul,

my loving being,

The love that is instilled in me

Even if you cannot see or understand the essence of me as a woman

I like who I am

Your hateful words mean **nothing to me**

They're just tears, right?

You gotta deal with my strange cuz I'm weird

Well, I gotta deal wit cha fear cuz you scared

But they're just tears, right?

You left me your heart; I guess I didn't touch it right

So maybe I should give it back and say f--- it, right?

They're just tears, right?

I'll erase the text messages; delete the voicemails as well

Back in your man cave is where you will go

Where no one can see you hurt alone

And to answer your question

Yes, they are just tears

Yours

There's a special something in living life

It's so special that if you added your mind's capacity

multiplied by gravity

it would never equate

Words you have none; your silence is empty; you have nothing to say

Invisible; hide your truth

bury it deep where no one can ever see

Can you dig where I dug? I go looking for giants while you stay on the run

too much for you to comprehend

You have algebraically mastered a way to get away, formulating

Adding the past to your present to only equal your future.

Step up; step down; make a choice

wear a frown it won't change your life

it will leave you stranded and behind, waiting for change you will never find

Run to the highest mountain, sift through the dirt on the ground your life and history will not be told or found

Like beginnings, life has **one ending**

Lonely in my heart like the desert without its sand

like a touch without hands

like a baby without a smile

like a guilty man who has had no trial

like the sun that feels so cold

like a gray-haired woman who is lonely and old

and I sit fully sane

of this feeling that I cannot explain

it is beyond any pain I have ever known

Hope

there is none

that is worse

Loneliness in my heart keeps me in tears

The beats have gotten softer; I can barely hear

Sometimes I can't even feel, my feelings have all disappeared

My words make no sense, but now it's part of my life

Love, smiles, and happiness never lived here

I hear my inner cries

This is not right, nor is it fair

Step by step in an unwanted space

Life is running me, and I have lost this race

It's over

Love of My Life

When I began dating, it was shortly after finishing grad school at Yale, a school that no one believes I even went to unless I show them my degree. Hmm. It's funny how even now I must prove myself to so many who don't believe a beautiful, strong black woman can finish at the top of her class summa cum laude with perks, including a brand-new car from Yale University.

However, let me stop bragging about myself only for a moment. It was really my dedication and the fact I slept, ate, and dated only school for three whole years. I did nothing but study my ass off. I stayed focused on my studies. My goal was to get across that stage with my degree in my hand, period. Even after I received my cap and gown and saw my name on the graduation roster, I was still not convinced. It was not until three weeks prior to graduation that I was sure that my heart would not be broken from this love affair I had with school.

Graduation day was exciting. It was the best way to end the relationship with the complete understanding that we grew apart. It was time to move on into the next phase of life. I realized my new relationship would not be considered a rebound and I could find someone that would give me conversation and maybe a nice dinner.

Six months after traveling the world, there I sat at a wonderful company that I landed by completing an internship the previous year. Never did I imagine the manager would keep his word and hire me once I graduated, but he did. Yes, this lady had her own office with her name on the door. I was super proud of myself. This is when my new life began. I remember that day so very well; I planned to one day tell my sons and daughters. My next goal was to have a fine ass husband and a team full of children. This is in fact how I met my soulmate the father of my many children.

His approach was not unusual, but original. He sent me an email, "Just wanted to say hello; would you like to have lunch at 12:30 today?" At the bottom of the email was a rose. Of course, I had no idea who this mystery man was, but I did know it had our company's name and logo at the bottom. This made me think it was someone at the firm, but that would be against policy. I thought, "It's just lunch. It's not like we are dating."

After thinking for a few seconds, I quickly responded before I changed my mind, "Yes, where would you like to meet?" His next response, "See you out in front. Just remember, this lunch is on me so don't bring anything except your beautiful smile." That was a little scary. How does he know I have a beautiful smile? Was he watching me, or has he sat across from me in our many board meetings? Who is this mystery man?

As I sat waiting patiently for lunch to come, mentally I scanned every male that worked in the firm. I could not think of one that I would want to go out to lunch with. I never considered that it could have been one of the pretty women that worked there. They were always giving me compliments and sending smiles my way. "Oh Lord, I pray it's not; I hate breaking hearts."

Right before meeting my mystery lunch date, I went to the ladies' room to freshen up and apply a little makeup. Giving myself the once over, I had a boss ass outfit on, fitting me like the queen I am. I was very confident in my appearance, as I headed to meet my lunch date.

As I stepped out the door, the first thing I saw was a white stretch limo and two handsome men standing in front of it. One was obviously the driver, but who was the fine black, chocolate brother standing next to him? This could not be my lunch date.

Before I could have another doubt or thought, he walked towards me and said, "Hello Miss Adams. I know it's a bit much, but my name is Donnell Young. I am that mystery lunch date you been trying to figure out. Shall we go?" The driver opened the door to let me in and then ran to the other side to open Donnell's door. All I could smell was fresh flowers, expensive wine, and a fragrance (some of the best smelling cologne I have ever encountered). I thought, "My goodness pinch me! This is not real!" This was the kind of stuff I've seen on television; however, I was going to enjoy every minute of it.

I could not even play it off as if I was used to this. Donnell saw my nervousness and discomfort. He immediately handed me a dozen roses and said, "Relax, we're going to have a great time," as he smiled and kissed my hand. He asked if I would like a glass of wine to start our lunch off. I immediately declined because I didn't want to go back to my office tipsy. Before I could get another word out, he said, "Oh, by the way, your boss is my ex-boss. He gave you the rest of the day off because he knows that you are an extraordinarily hard worker and have never been late or missed a day of work since you started working for the firm. Your work ethic is incredible."

He told me he used to work at the same firm before moving on to open his own firm, shortly after I was hired. Mr. Washington, my boss, was excited to invest in his idea of expanding the business. This "mystery man" had me figured out and mesmerized with his smile and voice. I quickly gathered my thoughts and stated, "Oh, well then, let's have a toast to you and me having the rest of the day off."

"So, Miss Adams, or is it okay that I call you Crystal?" I replied in the sweetest tone I could utter, "Of course, Donnell."

"What questions are running through that smart mind of yours? I know you have a few for me," Donnell said.

I answered, "I'm just curious, how do you know me and what made you choose me to take out to lunch out of all those beautiful women that work there?" I could smell the sweet minty fragrance of his breath mixed with the wine and his delightful cologne, as I watched the fullness of his lips reply.

He might have already guessed he had me where I have not been in years. All I wanted to do is inhale his every existence.

I found myself staring at this beyond fine chocolate man who had a set of pearly whites and a smile that made me just want to smile back. "Oh, the Lord has answered my prayers," was all I could think.

My number one weakness is a man with nice teeth, a great smile, sense of humor, and a masculine build. Oh yes, and large hands! My God, he had all these qualities. He said, "Well, I have been single for some time now. I worked at the firm for years and no one has ever peaked my interest. However, the first day you started at the firm, I watched you walk by my office with confidence and a well fitted red dress with the heals to match. You looked stunning. Besides your appearance, I noticed how genuinely nice you were to everyone, even the janitors. I was extremely impressed with your kindness. I really admire that about you because so many women that work there wear the profession on their sleeve and come across fake or snobbish. I'm just keeping it real."

"I must agree with you on that one," I chimed in. "I had to put a few people in their places for coming off that way to me. I'm glad you saw that I was different. I appreciate your honesty."

"Hey, Charles, can you play some Barry White, please, until we get to the restaurant? A strong baritone voice responded, "Sure can, boss."

We sat there admiring each other in an atmosphere that was filled with an aroma of pure harmony or maybe even lust. I don't even know. I just knew it was absolutely amazing what I was feeling.

"So, what's your deal? Why isn't a fine, successful man like yourself married with a whole slew of children? Wait, are you married? Do you have children?" With a little seductive grin, I stared straight at his face waiting to see that lie line that goes across all men's foreheads when they are trying to be dishonest.

Donnell just chuckled and got close, making me more vulnerable than I have already was feeling. He replied, "No. I have never been married and I don't have any children. Yes, I would love to do both. I hope I answered your questions. How about you? Would you like to get married and have all my children?" We both just laughed.

All I could say was, "I hope that wasn't a proposal, but to answer your question, yes, I would like to be married one day and I would love to have children, lots of them." No lie line on this handsome man's face appeared. I was ready to get brave and enjoy that bottom lip like it was my favorite piece of chocolate, but I pulled it together as I inched back just a little for my own sake.

"So, tell me about who Donnell is. What is it I need to know about you other than you want children and a wife?", I asked.

Donnell replied, "How about this, I will give you the lunch version and we can finish the story at dinner, that way you will have the opportunity to tell me more about you. Is that fair?"

"Dinner? Oh, we are really making this a real date. You sure you want to spend that much time with someone you don't know?", I asked. Without hesitation he said, "I absolutely do, but only if you want to spend that much time with me."

Jokingly I replied, "Sure, why not?"

It seemed like we had been driving forever. Donnell lowered the window on his side just enough so I could see his beautiful piece of land. I could tell because I saw a huge, beautiful colonial home sitting way off to the right with a long-extended driveway and several cars parked in it. It looked like a mansion compared to my two-bedroom condo. There was an amazing stream of water flowing close by. A table was set up, layered with a red, silk-like tablecloth, and white roses as the center piece. He even had a red runner with rose petals on both sides. It was exquisite! I could tell he took a lot of time to plan this and it obviously cost a lot of money. The money spent didn't impress me, but the fact that he chose me did. Four waiters were waiting to serve us even though it was obvious that it was just me and this handsome man.

Donnell said, "My lady, we have finally arrived. Let's get some lunch and continue this conversation." As the driver opened my door, Donnell was right there ready to take my hand. He escorted me to the table like a true gentleman and pulled out my seat, but not before I felt his sweet breath whisper in my ear, "You look amazing." That's it! Whatever happens from this point, I am not responsible for my actions. I am now officially horny, hot, and moist! It's been over five years since I even thought about sex or been intimate with anyone. Even though I made a vow to myself and maybe God that I would wait until marriage, I am having second thoughts. This is the first time in a long time that I have I felt so vulnerable and ready for whatever this man wants to do.

Donnell snapped me out of these thoughts by waving his hand towards the waiter. He immediately came over and asked me if I decided what I wanted to order. I hadn't even looked at the menu! My mind was stuck on this hunk of chocolate sitting in front of me, however, I played it off cool and said, "Oh, yes, may I have the Caesar salad with extra tomatoes and olives?" Donnell ordered the same with a side order of grilled shrimp and stuffed salmon.

As soon as the waiter disappeared, I said, "So Donnell, let's pick up where we left off. What's your deal? Why doesn't a fine man like you, well off, have a woman or man in your life? Donnell chuckled at my slight sense of humor, but reality is some men like both, so I had to kind of sneak that in there. I'm glad he found it funny because if he would have been defensive that would have been the first red flag of the day.

He said, "Well beautiful lady, first let me reassure you, I'm definitely not interested in the same sex. I don't have anything against it, but I do believe God has chosen my soulmate and queen to be a beautiful woman, like yourself. Secondly, to be honest, I'm looking to settle down with my soulmate and explore the rest of our lives together. Up until now, I have not met anyone, like I stated earlier in our conversation, that caught my attention like you have."

"Okay, well that was a great answer. You are not trying to be one of those brothers that 'hit it and quit it' and move on to the next one?"

"Absolutely not! I have more respect for myself and honestly, I want to make love, not have sex. There is a difference. With that being said, I have been abstinent for three years by choice. I will stay that way until I find my wife to share my sexual pleasures with. Would you like me to tell you more or would you like to save some of this conversation for dinner?"

Donnell could tell by the look on my face that I was amazed by every word that came out of his mouth. He spoke volumes to my whole being. I think my soul just got married. As he poured us both another glass of wine, I agreed to save the rest of the conversation for dinner.

We just chatted about our favorite movies and things we liked to do on our days off. We also talked about our families. I found out that Donnell was raised by a single father. His mother was diagnosed with a rare type of cancer and lost that battle when he was ten. His expression changed as he started telling me just how close they were. One thing he remembered the most from his mother was to always treat a woman with respect and to listen to his father because he was a good man.

His father and mother were together for twenty years. They both met in high school and went to the same college before getting married. He has no siblings, however, stated his mother had two miscarriages before he was born. He grew up pretty much alone. Sounds like my story, however, I was raised by a single mom. I lost my dad at twelve from a horrible car accident that left my mom in a wheelchair. I am also the only child but grew up very fast because I had to learn how to care for my mother. Thank God for a great aunt who was a doctor in my hometown. She taught me everything and left her job for two years to take care of my mom to get her motivated to at least want to go on with life. The doctors said she would never walk again. My aunt helped her learn to accept that and still enjoy her life.

Donnell and I lost someone in our lives that we really loved. I could see his pain was equal to mine and he didn't hold back his emotions as he told me the story of his mom's last days. We also talked about traveling to some of the same places as we chuckled and playfully touched each other now and then. I knew he was something special and God had orchestrated this part of our lives perfectly.

I knew her

Have you ever seen a woman so sad when she smiled it still looked like a frown?

I didn't know that could possibly be

Until it happened right in front of me

She stood there looking in my direction and said,

"I'm happy to see you"

Yet her face said, "I'm sad and lonely"

I wanted to change all that because of the way it made me feel

Her sadness and frown were contagious

Her spirit was shattered, her faith was lost

She needed to be found and broken pieces needed to be mended

My thoughts became full of fear of the impossible

Because I knew of her condition, I felt somewhat responsible

What am I supposed to do?

I had not one clue

I stayed around and chatted for a while

Making jokes with hope to make her smile

But all that remained was an upside-down smile

I gave her a hug before I left her, with the hopes of seeing her again

She hugged me tightly and asked if we could do this again

I smiled and cried at the same time, but nodded my head yes

Her final words were

"I don't know"

My response was

"What are you unsure about?"

She just smiled with her upside frown and said

"Life."

Negatives equal negative energy, lies, liars, trifling, hatred, racism, bigotry, confusion, sexism, depression, hateful words,

nigger, cracker, spick, KKK, skin heads, ideologies, swearing, cussing, alcohol, wine and spirits, drugs, hoes, sluts, hookers, pimps, prostitutes, lust, addiction, misconceptions, OG's, new G's, gangs, broken hearts, broken spirits, tears, pain, screams, abuse, murder, rapists, incest, greed, hunger, starvation.

There a is a God of this world who fell many years ago from being one of the best. He wanted the power of his creator. He became evil and took all good and made it bad. Satan, the devil, Lucifer, whatever name you choose is all the same. He is a liar and his purposes are to kill, steal, and destroy all of mankind. The best place for you to keep him is under your feet, stepping on his head, and crushing his lying mouth. He has destroyed many lives, and some have even sold their souls. **Don't let him get yours!**

Never found guilty for it, for this crime we all know of

Everyone knew one way or another, some from many miles

away

News flashes of another victim

and the man got away

Screams are the same no matter where they are as they are

being held down

being stripped of every type of dignity or pride that ever

existed

as the next victim takes his or her place, it becomes just

another rape case laying there

no need to fight guns have no arms

hope has no might

blood soon is gushing from every opening in their bodies as the penetration tears apart their mind and their hearts

with the gnashing of teeth, all you can hear is the devil's playground lurking near their flesh has been torn away screeching sounds of pain moaning, echoing throughout the world and all they can say is

"I can live another day, not after this.

My soul has been contaminated."

She told.

He did it. He told you it was him. You didn't believe them because of your connection with them. Your boyfriend, your girlfriend, your uncle, your friend; many disguises rape wears.

The victim never wins

Don't be fooled.

Rape does not discriminate.

It's sad to hear this truth.

The world ignores the victims' cries, the moans and groans, pain in their eyes.

This is heard loudly everywhere.

This demon has now taken a form of life, claiming its territory, lurking around in so many people's lives, waiting patiently to do what it knows best.

Life as a rape case, no trial, no jury.

Found not guilty.

Yours, no longer mine

Your thoughts have impaired my reality

Come, have a seat and taste my pain

Through these fogged glasses and cold hands

Touching you from my frozen heart

Passing those unwanted spirits that are only there to tear you

apart

The one that torments me, and now you

The unwanted, unloved, forever lonely

What a bliss to hold such thought, such reality

impaired thoughts

It was part of my life

Yours, no longer mine

Goodbye darkness

You haven't walked in my shoes

you haven't been through what I have been through

you have not trodden that rocky road of child abuse,

poverty, and incest, or have you?

What do you know about my shoes?

What do I know about yours?

My shoes are torn and worn; two sizes too small

My feet ache like my heart and spirit every day

They are swollen and bruised, overwhelmed with pain

These are my shoes

I have worn them every day

the only ones I ever had

the only ones I ever knew

Even with all those steep hills and high mountains I have

climbed

these shoes of mine were never kind

I was pushed and shoved, falling harder to the ground each time

Only light shines in the holes of my shoes

In darkness, I have learned to stride

this light helps me find my way through

I'm looking for a shoemaker to give me a new pair

these are worn and torn

tight on my feet

can't take any more

they scream loudly in pain and agony

every day I must endure

I'm done, I decided no more

Just when I thought it was over

He crept in one more time

I wasn't asleep thoughts running quickly through my mind

run, run, run in those shoes of mine

I found myself lying naked and cold as he tore through my

spirit but never touching my soul

My only choice was to live or die

I made my way out of that bloody mess that poured out of

my body

Put on my dress

and my holey shoes, grimy with old blood stains this is all I

had

Found a moldy piece of bread and a half a bottle of water

It was time to go

Where? I had no clue

nor did I care

I wanted to get out of there

These shoes I'm trotting in are full of pain

They need to be replaced not repaired

In search of a shoemaker, who I am determined to find

And when I do, I will be leaving these shoes and the pain

they come with

far behind

When I was in the world, I got disrespected by myself and many others

While there, I also got lied on and told many lies

Got completely wrapped up in negativity

Felt like I was becoming a nobody

after believing that, my looks became uglier and uglier to me and everyone else

I used to think I was beautiful, pretty, or at least attractive

not any more

I have become completely in sin

developed a low self-esteem

became envious of everyone else around me

Bought material things to make me feel better

that didn't work anymore

After the dark settled, I was crying every day because I hated life and myself most of all.

The day finally came when I felt like I didn't want to live anymore.

I only smiled when I thought about dying

I felt a sense of happiness knowing that I no longer had to endure the pain and suffering I allowed the world to make me a part of

I knew I wasn't strong enough or brave enough to complete suicide

So now what?

Maybe I can change!

Maybe I can find the true me again

Maybe, just maybe, this is truly just the end.

As so many close their eyes on the lost souls, hurt beings, or

little girls and boys stuck in a time with shattered hopes,

never ending nightmares

They come one by one holding broken pieces of their lives,

needing and wanting to know who they are

I carefully handled one piece at a time

Gently reminding them that in order to heal their

foundation, they must leave the past in the past

begin again

one must start fresh

A place of healing, repairing, forgiveness

Put all the broken pieces back together again

Pieces that were shattered, but not missing

Find one's soul and renew one's mind

The line was long and one by one they came seeking help

With their broken pieces, wet with tears

minds shattered; hearts filled with fears

I took one at a time

Prayed that God would help with each and everyone

Two hands, one heart

Broken pieces, someone's sons, someone's daughters

Family Ties

Hello, let me introduce you to TRI. We are using abbreviations to protect the identity of each person until we have someone who is willing to reveal his or her name.

She is 18 years old. Her back story is simple, yet complex. She has been in the system since she was fifteen. Her mother left her with an aunt at the age of twelve. Her biological mother was addicted to drugs. There are several police reports of domestic violence between her mother and a man who she called her uncle. TRI recalls witnessing sexual and physical abuse.

While in the care of her aunt, there were allegations of abuse made. Child Protective Services was called three times. It became clear in my mind that it was just another money-making business. However, the fourth time CPS was called, a worker found that the client had sustained serious physical injuries. Finally, she was removed and has been in the state's custody since!

She reported that she had been raped by her aunt's boyfriend and other men that her aunt knew. She stated that she remembered seeing money exchange afterwards. The assaults started shortly after her mother left her there. She also stated that she witnessed the violence against her mother which was why she never fought back or told anyone, but she wanted to.

She realized she was the price for the debt her mother owed and that she was sold to the aunt to pay that debt. Medical records showed she was pregnant at age thirteen. The client reported to the doctors that she had some form of abortion. All she remembered was there was a lot of blood and pain. She was also told she better not tell anyone, or they would kill her babysitter. The botched abortion damaged her ovaries. She will never be able a to have a child. Initially, she was not sad about it. Later, she realized she was robbed of the opportunity to be a mother. On the flip side, she thought it was good because she wouldn't be able to create another monster like her. Her words.

Another one. She suffers from low self-esteem and started seeing a mental health counselor at the age seventeen. She is now turning eighteen and has been in group homes and foster homes since she was four. She stated that she was verbally abused by staff, in two of the foster homes she lived. She stated that other residents spit on her, poured a bottle of perfume in her hair, alienated her from other family members, and forced her to eat scraps from their plates. She reported she had to clean the entire kitchen and was also locked in a bathroom for two hours. She had an Individualized Education Plan or IEP, read at a six-grade level, loved school, but hated all her teachers. She was one of the few that made it to the 12th grade and even thought about college. She worried about her Post Traumatic Stress Disorder or PTSD. She was also concerned because her social skills were limited. She felt defeated before she even started.

Next up is someone's daughter. She was not taught proper hygiene skills. She reported she does not like the smell of cologne or perfume because her abuser wore lots of cologne and would make her wear perfume before raping her. Per her report, her abuser was attracted to her because of her beautiful hair. She reported she wears hats now to cover balding. She was nineteen years old before she saw any kind of physician, male or female. She reported she does not like to be in the presence of any type of male authority figures. If she were, she would only speak when spoken to or would remain silent depending on the tone of that person. She was diagnosed with Post Traumatic Stress Disorder but did not start counseling until two years after the assault. She would have extreme meltdowns and leave a room when she felt overwhelmed.

Another young woman, she began puberty while in junior high school. Her developed "woman parts" were enticing to her basketball coach. He sexually assaulted her while she was showering in the girls' locker room. The very first time he raped her he held a gun to her head and threatened to kill her whole family if she told anyone. Of course, she believed him. She didn't have a reason not to believe him. She became his sex slave for the next five months. *A fellow student caught him and reported him to the school officials. She also reported an incident that she witnessed between him and a young man. The young man took his life last year, but no one ever knew why. They do now.*

Her parents did not feel they could handle the changes that occurred in their daughter because of the incident. They signed her over to the state because she had severe behavior issues and difficulty completing daily tasks, such as bathing every day. She remembered the day they picked her up in the state car. Her mother didn't even show any emotion. She told her it was for the best and hoped she would get the help needed. She left with a case manager and was taken to her first group home.

Another broken piece. He was born a male trapped in a female body because his mother raised him as a female. Now, at the age twenty, he is not sure who he is. "Yes, I have an uncircumcised penis," he said. "To me it looks like a vagina. Yes, I was taught to sit down to pee. I am clearly not attracted to women. Well, at this point, I'm not attracted to anyone. I do know that both of my parents died before I turned sixteen.

My mom, who I was really close to, died from cancer. I was with her, until the state took me, the year before she died. My dad was abusive to me and my mom. My mom thought that I would have a better life if she just gave me to the state. Right after that, I was told my dad died of an overdose. I have one older brother. I thought he was my boyfriend because he was the first one to introduce me to all kinds of sex when I was ten years old. He didn't live in the rundown cold house with me and my mom, but my mother addressed him by his first name. She never told me that was my brother. She would say just listen to whatever he tells you to do. I guess that meant everything, including oral sex when he wanted it. He taught me how to do it right and told me I could make that a career goal. She knew what he was doing to me. I think she was afraid of him because he was a big, strong man. He was ten years older than me. My mom had him when she was only fourteen. I did witness him taking her money out of her pocketbook, yelling in her face, and calling her names you should never call your mother.

Can you help? Here are all the broken pieces. I think! These are true stories of daughters and sons lost in a system that has set them up for failure. Without someone to help them repair these broken pieces, they will stay broken.

Where I stand is where I have chosen to be

Learning how to love me

Not allowing others to influence my thoughts

Anger, disappointments, abandonment issues just to name a few

Putting each one in its proper place

left behind

No longer do I have to think of the unkind

My happiness I control; my loneliness only I can foretell

My destiny is not based on those things that come and go, but

I awoke believing in the here and now

This is what I will make of each minute

as I complete this task, I slowly move towards the now

Now will lead me to the end

so now, I can begin again

To start at a place I haven't been before, learning to prosper even more

Relying on my father for his guidance

this will get me further

One day at a time; one hour as it passes

I have finally arrived

It's so nice to see that love still lives in me

That I can answer the tears of others

As they trust in me to reach out with caring arms

Drawing them near me, I touch their souls

Submitting myself so they can touch mine

I've learned how to do this

From the love I once lost

But it was never forgotten

The things that have passed

reaching within myself the seeds planted

Right there in the center of my heart

Watered by the spirit of God

Cultivated by His mercy and grace

Even with my tears that I have cried

Those feelings of loss and despair, I prayed away

Love is a feeling that is truly real

Until you learn to give it away, you will never know

The abundance of it all

Your love can change someone's life

In ways you will never know

Until you give your love away

Remember, you are **not lost or forgotten.**

If there was no name to call

Hello, Mr. White Man

I have several questions I need to ask

Why do you hate me so?

Is it because I'm so dark you can't see anything but the color

of my skin?

You don't want to find out what kind of human being that I

am inside?

If there was no name to call

Hey, Mr. Black Man

How could I get to see who you are inside or who you claim

to be

if you think that I am like all the white people

that seem to hate you?

You are more like them

Hey, Mr. White Man

How can I not think in such a way when for hundreds of

years

my people were enslaved

by your unfair rules and laws that don't protect me or my

people?

Your history does not teach the truth

It's filled with lies

If there were no names to call...

Our history is more than just name calling

from nigger, spade, coon

Now, I'm just black

You tried and succeeded

to change our names from kings and queens

which we came from

On your ships loaded up one by one

Your history is not our **true story**

Is there such thing as change?

Can I see my true goals in life?

Is love such a word?

Do things get better?

Will a smile ever come upon my face?

Will my questions ever be answered?

Yes, my child, with the power that I have stored inside you

I can make you brand new

Give you a clean spirit

And your goals in life shall be accomplished

Love is something you already have in your heart

With my love, comes everlasting happiness

A friend for life is who I will always be

Never will I change always me

Then you will begin to see that things will only get better

Smiles will overflow on your beautiful face

With the thought that I am always there

Someone who cares

At any time, as the world spins, day by day

You can ask me any questions

I will be your guardian angel, a friend for life

His name is Jesus Christ

She is so beautiful, especially the parts of her you have never

seen

Look into her eyes, you will see her soul

Beyond what some perceive as her selfless mind

She is beautiful

Her kindness and her beauty would never fade

When you see her sashay across the room

close your mouth

as your mind races to that thought,

she is not a snack

but a good, delicious meal

Every inch of her being is simply delightful

curved in the perfect image of beauty

inside and out

This morning came so fast

I was already wishing the day and time would have passed

Getting ready was no problem at all

Getting there was my downfall

Of course, I went anyway

on a dare and a prayer

Finally, as I reached my new job to be

Something terrible inside disturbed and frightened me

it was my nerves running in all directions

I couldn't keep track

As I walked slowly, taking baby steps

There they were all in one big room

Some with somewhat pleasant faces and some not

As I got the all-American body stare with some looks of

surprise

nerves took over

I didn't know what to say or do

There was a tall man looking in my direction

As he spoke and said, "hello," I said, "hi"

He directed me with a point of a finger

"This is the work and what you will do

follow the instructions"

Right after that he was through

I sat there like a new pair of shoes trying to stay focused

On reading the tiny print on what I needed to do

I had no one to impress with my skills

It was time to show them all my intelligence

Hired for a reason

I was the perfect person for the job

As I enter another day in this world of bliss

Knowing what life has in store for me

it pulls my inner soul, guiding me to only think

I might have a chance to find happiness, maybe even some

peace

Every day I take notice of my mental pain

As life strikes me with a blood ridden sword of life

With nothing but a thought that only misleads

Today or tomorrow, will not be my end

Only strength I have left is within my heart

Holding on as I feed off someone else's happiness

Only life can conquer itself

In the end, the creator will win

Yet life doesn't cease striking me harder than yesterday

As my blood splatters about making me weak

No need for me to give up because life takes no prisoners

For its evil spirit thrives on pain

It lusted for blood

it's the only reason

There is only one way to destroy this thing, this sword

as it is striking

I have learned through my weakness

I must now learn to strike

Take back the sword of life

Drive it into itself

Miraculous

Fascinating

His presence is irresistible

As it leads my every desire to shiver and quake

I have no idea who this man possibly could be

He must be someone special

not just to me

As I watch him day after day

He leaves his footprint in my mind in a mysterious way

I am so curious to find out more about him

When he speaks, his words are so strong and sweet

His body is impressive

every muscle carved magnificently

I'm finding a way to get his attention other than in my imagination

Not quite sure just how

So much I don't know and the what ifs are keeping me at bay

Don't know what I will say

I want to get to know him in every way

Mysterious man, I pray you stay

A child who has had a rough life

prays to someday

be a good wife

All the rough spots she has been through, all the lies and

abuse

she felt

Every day the scars are reminders

"Why me?" is the question she constantly asks herself

every day

As she grows up

finding herself

she keeps making the wrong turns in this thing called life

So confused

her mind wanders

she stays lost

Life, to her, is mysterious

she believes no one cares

It's like a puzzle with so many missing parts

Yet she keeps searching

Away from pain

a healed heart

I was in love for two hours

scared of what my heart felt

It was him who made me feel so good

So wanted

So loved

Someday real soon

Those hours went by so slowly in my mind

Only thinking of him

Trying to taste every inch of his sweet lips

The warmth of his strong embrace, feeling love

wrapped around me, which felt so good

I opened my eyes and saw his handsome face

when he began to speak

I was terrified of the words he would say

It's time, it's time for me to go away

It's time to end this day

Remember, I love you

Oh, how it hurts!

The pain continues to linger

It feels so bad! It goes beneath the depths of my heart

Now, all I hold on to

and remain to say is

you hurt me too

And you say, "Never have I walked out on you,

leaving you with nothing but gray skies and tears in your

eyes.

For whatever pain I have caused,

never did I hesitate to make it up to you

in whatever way you wanted to."

Every time the tears flow inside my soul

I feel betrayed, left to suffer,

as if I was never part of your loving heart

Never did I know that pain could hurt so bad

Someone you loved

Giving yourself to

day and night

I kept telling myself this emptiness inside was not real

Neither were these stains from my tears

Is this so-called love beyond repair?

Rhetorical

Broken

My mother graduated from Boston College with a degree in business. She was an extremely smart and intelligent woman. She came a long way from being a teenage mother, someone who grew up in a group home, and a high school dropout. However, that didn't stop her from pursuing her goals. She loved children and wanted to help every child she could.

She was not just astonishingly smart, but she was also amazingly beautiful. My mother had a full figure and was very stylish. She was always getting compliments from other women and me. She took her talents and invested in building the first daycare in a low-income community. She helped other single mothers by mentoring them and their children. Even though we no longer lived in that area, my mother made sure she continued to give back by working there and helping others.

My father was her soulmate. He stuck by her side since day one. They were only two years apart in age. Growing up as a teen father was not an easy task for him either. Fortunately for him, he was able to finish high school. He had no desire to attend college but was a smart man who went to trade school to do what he loved most which was driving trucks and construction. My father was very well built, dark, and very handsome. I was happy when people told me I looked like my dad. I never saw him angry. He always had a positive word to say and was always smiling. His smile was contagious. He was often mistaken by women as a flirt. My mother was so secure she never let it bother her. They were together so long, and he was still bringing home the money and the honey. I believe my father cherished my mother. He loved her and was not afraid to protect his wife.

Right before I entered high school, my father finished building our home. We moved in during my freshman year. My mom enjoyed decorating every single room in the house, including mine and my siblings' rooms. Even though it was just me and my two younger sisters at home, my dad made sure that we all had our own bedroom plus a guest room. Of course, there plenty of bathrooms and even a full wet room and family room.

Let me introduce the rest of the family. There were my brothers Nick and Charles (a.k.a Chuck) who was named after my great uncle. I heard so many amazing stories about Uncle Chuck. Then there was my twin sister, Tayana (Tee), brother, Thomas (Tom Tom) and Maxine (Mackey) was the oldest girl. We all had nick names. Kevin is the oldest child, but we called him Junior. He was named after our dad.

Reading this intro, it sounds like my family had it all together. Who could ask for anything more? As we all know, life can sometimes take you on a serious road trip. Tragedy struck my family. My sister was killed three months after moving into what we thought was a safe neighborhood. I remember this day very well. I was headed to my first period class when I was called down to the office. There, I met my mother and sisters with the counselor, Miss Anderson. Their eyes were bloodshot from crying.

"What happened? What's going on?" I asked. "It's the twins and dad. They were on their way to school when they were in a terrible car accident. Tom Tom and your father are both in critical condition. You sister may not live, she is on life support."

Miss Anderson saw my face as I went into complete shock. She gently sat me down. My mom and sister began to sob. Shortly after, we left school and went to the hospital. The doctors met us in the hallway and delivered the bad news that my sister died. She stopped breathing. The machine could no longer help her. The trauma she suffered was too much. I found out later that the car slammed into the side my sister was sitting on. The other driver was speeding. The impact was so hard my dad's car flipped three times and ejected my father and brother. My sister's chest cavity was crushed.

My dad and brother survived, but they weren't unscathed. They both had broken ribs, head contusions, and broken arms and legs. They both remained in the hospital for weeks. My brother had to learn how to walk again and didn't really talk as much as he used to for the first four months after the passing of my sister. Burying my sister was the worst experience I have ever been through. I was only sixteen and I lost someone I loved. My heart was shattered. I could only imagine how my parents were feeling.

My mother was a very God-fearing mother who didn't believe in religion; however, she was dedicated to helping lost souls. She taught all her children that the most important relationship in this world is with God. My mother would pray day and night for our family, saved and unsaved. She reminded us everyday to remember to give thanks for everything including the air we breathe. This tragedy didn't really change her feelings about God, but I could hear her in her prayer closet yelling at God asking him why he took her baby. Shortly after I would her say, "Lord, please know I give you praise as you continue to heal my family through this tough time." My mother prayed like this consistently at the same time every day for the next two years. I was mad at God. I didn't know how to process what happened. There was nothing anyone could say at that time to convince me to change how I felt. I stopped going to school and had no intention of going back. I wasn't even thinking about graduation. I honestly stopped caring about everything.

My dad recovered well, however; he was battling with Post Traumatic Stress Disorder (PTSD) bad. He would wake up crying and screaming for both of my siblings. My mother would just lay hands on him and begin to pray until he either was calm or went back to sleep. I could tell when she had a bad night with my dad and was up praying all night. She would give the daycare over to Mrs. Clara to run because she was mentally and physically tired. She was tired of caring for all the grieving and hurting people in her life. Things only got worse before they got better.

My dad went into a deep depression. He would not get out of bed, eat, or even socialize with the family. My twin brother who survived was a lot better than all of us. He encouraged my mom by saying that God was going to make dad better and that our family would be okay. My brother and sister moved back into help my mother take care of the family that was really hanging on by a prayer. Kevin Jr. nurtured my father back to health. He helped bathe him, dress him, and started taking long walks with him. They started spending a lot of time together and even got my dad to flash that beautiful smile again. I thank God for my family, especially my brother,

Kevin Jr. He was a praying man who adopted the same strength and faith my mother had. I never saw two stronger people in my whole life. He was a spitting image of my father and he had the ability to make you smile when you felt like crying. My sister, Maxine, was able to convince me to go back to school after home schooling me for four months and praying alongside my mom for our family. I could no longer feel like I was making things worse.

My anger wasn't as strong but at times, I thought I heard my sister's voice. It would make me sad. I realized that I shouldn't be sad because her voice was a delight to hear. Not everything was going well after ten months of hurt, trauma, and devastation, but things were certainly looking better for me and my family. I was able to get right back on track with school and double my classes. I was taking ninth and tenth grade classes with the ability to go straight in eleventh grade. I dedicated every success to my bright and beautiful sister, who I still miss today. Tom Tom was doing extremely well. He, too, was already back in school. He would not ride in a car without a helmet, but one day at dinner he said, "Momma, sissy told me I didn't need the helmet anymore. She will be my guardian angel."

Silence covered the room like a thick fog. My father said to him, "That is good news son. She is mine, too. Even though we miss her, she remains in our hearts." Since we were all sharing good news, my brother chimed in and stated, "Well, I started a scholarship in Tayana's name. The first award will be given out this coming school year to three freshman students of our choice who will be attending the local community college. I have been working on this since she passed. I have raised over fifty thousand dollars, thanks to our neighbors, church, and family for all the donations. We can come together as a family to choose the perfect candidates and present them with the scholarship at our first annual scholarship award event. What do you guys think?"

My mom and sister screamed with excitement, "Praise God! That is excellent news!" My dad said, "Amen, I agree." Tom Tom said, "Yes, Tee would be proud of us all honoring her name this way! I'm in! I can't wait to pick the lucky students!"

"Well, I have good news as well." Everyone turned and looked at my dad who had not driven or been back to work in two years. He stated he would be shopping for a new car and would be back running his construction business again the following week. Everyone in the house busted into praise. It felt like we were having church right at our dining room table and God was pastoring the whole thing. What an amazing day! My family would never be whole again, but one thing was for sure, if we had God running things, we would always be a family.

Where you may be

Wherever I may go

We are one

One times one, shall always equal one

If I am in a desert, you are there, too

If you are on top of a mountain

There I will be with you

I love you, girl

I will go to the end of the world for you

I will swim in a raging sea

With the hopes you would do the same for me

If I dream at night, you are the one that's on my mind

I know if you seek then you will find me

Right here with you, we are one

Feel me touch you with my soul

I feel when you touch me and it makes me whole

I didn't see your face; I just heard your voice

it was love at first glance

It was your heart that put me in a trance

My heart connected as one on love's horizon

I won't leave because we are one

Shine on, crazy diamond, shine on

If you get there before me

Remember, we are one

You and I are becoming one

As we seek to find the true meaning of love

Hand in yours

one heartbeat

single sound of two people in love

I got here before you did

Now, I sit shining

Amongst the mist of very time you held me close

In my heart, I want to be closer

Two hearts to become a single beat

You kept my heart from feeling any fears

You wiped away all my hurt

you kissed my tears,

Captivating me every time unceasingly,

Filling my spirit with your security of strength

I believe you are in love with me, as I am with you

Through the storms, our diamond will shine on

You and I together, as one, seeking to find this eternal love

This is us together as one

Until the end of the world

No surrender, no retreat

In this hand, I hold a fistful of questions

Is this what I need within this concrete I dwell

Or shall I say, in this life that is a living hell?

Taught this way to be so easily dispelled and inside my spirit,

all I can do is yell

Then, when I look, I see that I hold the key to my true

destiny

Your eyes only show a reflection of me

that's all I can see

Your promise to me is that I would forever be free

No felony, just life is what it is meant to be

I now hold my head up high and scream

damn to defeat

All the while, sticking to this theory

No surrender, no retreat

Darkness of life allows you to find your way in the dark

Truth in understanding, knowledge, and strength to confront your every sin

Is this a concept of your every thought?

This way of life that cannot be sold, stolen, or brought

Many lives have been lost and battles we have fought

Only to seek out understanding or just how to keep it real

I'm done

my flesh can no longer feel

Dying daily asking to love and to heal

No surrender, no retreat

I hope you enjoyed my debut book, *Silence, No More.* I also hope you were inspired. I would love to hear your feedback.

Feel free to reach out and connect with me.

Visit www.lizmoore.me for more from Liz Moore.

www.ingramcontent.com/pod-product-compliance
Lightning Source LLC
Chambersburg PA
CBHW031652040426
42453CB00006B/278